Dinosaur's Day

FIRST EDITION
Project Editor Deborah Murrell; **Art Editor** Catherine Goldsmith; **US Editor** Regina Kahney;
Pre-Production Producer Nadine King; **Producer** Sara Hu; **Picture Researcher** Frances Vargo;
Picture Librarian Sally Hamilton; **Jacket Designer** Natalie Godwin;
Publishing Manager Bridget Giles; **Reading Consultant** Linda Gambrell PhD

THIS EDITION
Editorial Management by Oriel Square
Produced for DK by WonderLab Group LLC
Jennifer Emmett, Erica Green, Kate Hale, *Founders*

Editors Grace Hill Smith, Libby Romero, Michaela Weglinski;
Photography Editors Kelley Miller, Annette Kiesow, Nicole DiMella;
Managing Editor Rachel Houghton; **Designers** Project Design Company; **Researcher** Michelle Harris;
Copy Editor Lori Merritt; **Indexer** Connie Binder; **Proofreader** Larry Shea;
Reading Specialist Dr. Jennifer Albro; **Curriculum Specialist** Elaine Larson

Published in the United States by DK Publishing
1745 Broadway, 20th Floor, New York, NY 10019

Copyright © 2023 Dorling Kindersley Limited
DK, a Division of Penguin Random House LLC
22 23 24 25 26 10 9 8 7 6 5 4 3 2 1
001-333368-May/2023

A catalog record for this book
is available from the Library of Congress.
HB ISBN: 978-0-7440-6569-5
PB ISBN: 978-0-7440-6570-1

DK books are available at special discounts when purchased in bulk for sales promotions, premiums,
fundraising, or educational use. For details, contact: DK Publishing Special Markets,
1745 Broadway, 20th Floor, New York, NY 10019
SpecialSales@dk.com

Printed and bound in China

The publisher would like to thank the following for their kind permission to reproduce their images:
a=above; c=center; b=below; l=left; r=right; t=top; b/g=background
Alamy Stock Photo: Jeannie Burleson 12clb, 30cla; **Getty Images / iStock:** Warpaintcobra 12b;
Shutterstock.com: Computer Earth 4-5, 10-11, 29

Cover images: *Front:* **Dreamstime.com:** Natuska; **Getty Images / iStock:** TrishaMcmillan cr; *Back:* **Getty Images:** Sciepro cr

All other images © Dorling Kindersley
For more information see: www.dkimages.com

For the curious
www.dk.com

Dinosaur's Day

Ruth Thomson

Contents

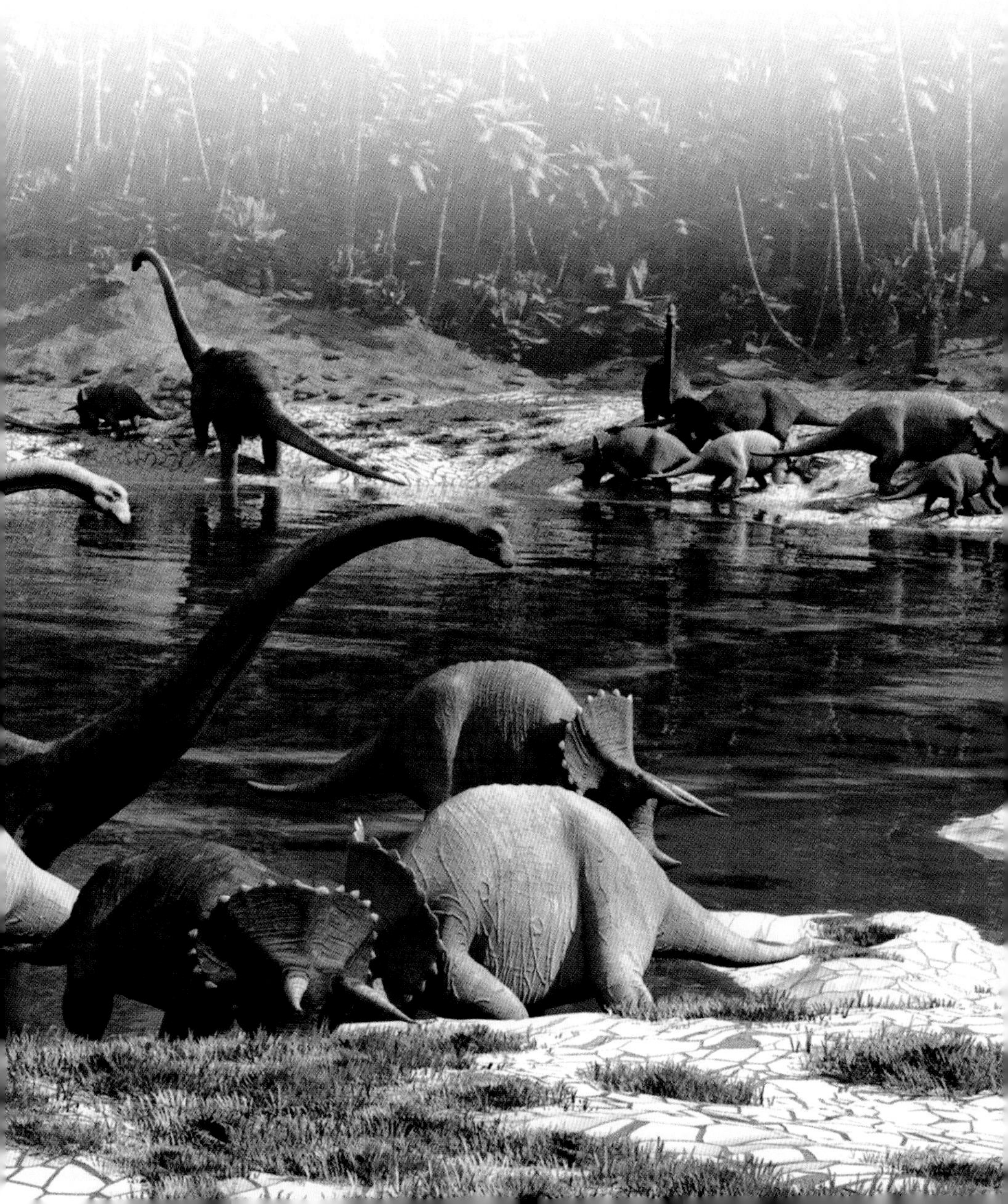

Meet the Triceratops

I am a dinosaur.
I am big and strong.

Triceratops
[try-SER-uh-tops]

I have horns
on my head.
I have a bony frill
on my neck.

frill

I look fierce,
but I am
gentle.

beak

I spend all day
eating plants.
I snip off twigs
and leaves with
my hard beak.

I live in a group called a herd. We look out for hungry dinosaurs. They might want to eat us!

Other dinosaurs
live near the river
with us.

Everything is quiet.
All of a sudden,
what do I see?

Watch Out for the T. rex!

The fiercest dinosaur
of all!
He has short arms
with sharp claws.
He has a huge mouth
full of sharp teeth.

claws

Tyrannosaurus rex
[tie-RAN-uh-SORE-us]

Another herd spots
the T. rex, too.
They run away on
their long legs.
They hide in the forest.

Ornithomimus
[OR-ni-thoh-MY-mus]

The duck-billed
dinosaurs stop eating.
They watch the T. rex.
If he comes too close,
they will run away.

bill

Edmontosaurus
[ed-MON-tuh-SORE-us]

The dinosaur with a big head sniffs the air.
He can smell the T. rex.
He will also run away if it comes too close.

Pachycephalosaurus
[PAK-ee-SEF-uh-low-SORE-us]

The dinosaurs with head crests hoot in alarm.

Parasaurolophus
[par-uh-sore-OLL-uh-fuss]

crest

Dinosaur in Danger

I watch the other
dinosaurs.
I forget to stay
with my herd.

I can see the T. rex.
He can see me.

The T. rex runs
toward me.
He looks hungry.

teeth

His mouth is open.
I can see his sharp teeth.

Thud!
Thud!

He comes
closer.

He stands up.
He is very tall.
He lifts his
head and roars
loudly.

He is trying to scare me.
But I am not scared.

I lower my head.
I roar back.
I will try to scare
him by shaking my
head and showing
off my big horns.

horns

The T. rex tries to bite me
with his sharp teeth.
I am still not scared.
I kick up the dust.
The T. rex gives up
and walks
away.

The T. rex is getting tired.
He stops fighting.
Now I am safe.

I am glad to be back
with my herd by the river.
The other dinosaurs come
back to the river, too.
They eat quietly.
I hope the T. rex won't
come back again.

Glossary

beak
a narrow, pointed end of a Triceratops's mouth

claws
hard and sharp ends of the T. rex's arms, used for slashing prey

crest
a body part that curves over some dinosaurs' heads

frill
a bony part of a Triceratops's neck

horns
sharp points made from bone that stick out of some dinosaurs' heads

Index

Quiz

Answer the questions to see what you have learned. Check your answers with an adult.

1. What does a Triceratops eat?

2. What is a group of dinosaurs called?

3. Which fierce dinosaur makes the other dinosaurs run away?

4. What does a Triceratops use to fight a T. rex?

5. Imagine if you were a dinosaur for a day. What would you eat? Would you have any special features?

1. Plants 2. A herd 3. Tyrannosaurus rex or T. rex
4. Its horns 5. Answers will vary